Notre Dame Inspirations

Notre Dame Inspirations

The University's Most Successful
Alumni Talk About Life, Spirituality,
Football—and Everything Else
Under the Dome

Hannah Storm

Edited by Sabrina Weill

Doubleday, New York

This book is dedicated
to everyone who loves the
University of Notre Dame
(especially the whole
Storen clan).

PUBLISHED BY DOUBLEDAY
Copyright © 2006 by
Hannah Storm and Sabrina Weill
All Rights Reserved

Published in the United States by Doubleday, an
imprint of The Doubleday Broadway Publishing
Group, a division of Random House, Inc., New York.
www.doubleday.com

DOUBLEDAY and the portrayal of an anchor
with a dolphin are registered trademarks of
Random House, Inc.

Please see pages 174–176 for photo credits.

Cataloging-in-Publication Data is on file
with the Library of Congress.
ISBN-13: 978-0-385-51812-3
ISBN-10: 0-385-51812-9

Printed in China

10 9 8 7 6 5 4 3 2 1
FIRST EDITION

Contents

Preface

The experience of putting this book together has been amazing—I am so delighted to be able to share my conversations with all of the incredible people you're about to meet. The lessons they learned at Notre Dame have shaped their success, and it's clear to me that Notre Dame made it possible for these special people to achieve so much and to contribute so significantly to our world. I know you're going to enjoy their voices, their stories, and their Notre Dame memories, revelations, and inspirations.

Opposite: Students on campus, 1939.

Notre Dame Inspirations

"If you're going to be the center of attention no matter what, don't try to blend in— *shine*."

Hannah Storm
Class of 1983

My dad was always a huge Notre Dame fan. He had the school flag flying in front of our house every football Saturday. Nonetheless, I was planning to go to Duke University until we went one night to a dinner for the Atlanta-Notre Dame alumni club. Basketball coach Digger Phelps happened to be the speaker. My dad sidled up to Digger and said, "Hannah's thinking about going to Duke." Digger set his sights on me as if I was some kind of blue-chip basketball recruit, and essentially gave me the full-on Digger Phelps pitch! After that, I literally went home that night and signed my letter of intent to go to Notre Dame. Digger always jokes that he is the reason I went to Notre Dame . . . even though I'd never played basketball outside of our driveway!

What my dad knew, and what I came to appreciate, is there's so much great

"Conversations about life and its meaning— that's what makes Notre Dame so special."

Hannah Storm, 1983, *Dome Yearbook*.

tradition at Notre Dame. The university has offered the same core values and inspiration to generations of grads: service to others, a strong sense of community, and something that really can't be overstated—school spirit. When you say you went to the University of Notre Dame, you always get a reaction of some sort. It's great to have a degree from a school that everyone has heard of. It's part of your heritage. You say, "Well, I'm part English. I'm part German. I'm part Irish. And I'm a Domer."

During my years at Notre Dame, I really took full advantage of all that the school had to offer. I worked at the campus radio station as a DJ. That was a total blast. I also had a sports talk show my sophomore year, which I think only my roommates actually listened to. I was in a musical—*Pippin*. And later I began my TV career as an intern and sometime sports feature reporter at WNDU-TV.

There were also challenges. In the early eighties, we were still at the beginning stages of women attending Notre Dame. So it could be socially awkward at times. I remember, when the girls would get ice cream in the cafeteria, some of the less enlightened young men would actually "moo" at us as if we were going to turn into cows! But I have to say the experience of being occasionally teased and tortured really toughened me up. When I graduated and went into the completely male-dominated field of sports, I was prepared!

As women, we were such anomalies at Notre Dame, and that taught me to just go with that feeling. I thought, "I'm going to stick out like a sore thumb no matter what, so I'm not going to even try to blend in." So even though there were difficult moments, it was actually freeing in a way. If you're going to be the center of attention no matter what, don't try to blend in—*shine.*

Like so many others finding their way through those formative college years, I found a lot of comfort and solace in the spiritual aspect of Notre Dame. It was everywhere: in the dorm, in service activities, and at the Grotto. Spirituality was front and center in our lives. I'll never forget a great conversation with Father Mark Poorman, who was rector of Dillon Hall, a couple of

Hannah Storm (third from left) and friends at a Dillon Hall party in 1983.

years after graduation. My younger brother had just graduated and was about to go off to work with war refugees in Asia. I was in radio at the time, spinning records and doing sportscasts. I said to Father Poorman— because being at Notre Dame makes you think about these really profound life questions—"Well, Father, I feel like my brother is off saving the world, but what about me? I feel good about using my talents and I'm pushing ahead even though nobody wanted to hire me in sports because I'm a woman. But am I

Hannah Storm at the 2004 Democratic Convention with Rudy Giuliani.

really making a difference?" Father Poorman replied, "You know, Hannah, you're going to have a great platform. People are going to watch you and they're going to listen to you. You're in the public eye and you can set a good example by the way you live. You can make a huge difference." And you know what, he was right. (He'll tell you he usually is!)

That short talk with Father Poorman has stayed with me for my whole career, as I have strived to do things the right way and to be a good example. I did end up being considered a trailblazer for young women, teaching them to not be afraid to go into careers that are male-dominated. I feel really proud of that, and in a subtle way perhaps that has had a positive impact on the world. Those kinds of conversations that take place at Notre Dame, conversations about life and its meaning, are a key part of what makes Notre Dame so special.

Hannah Storm is co-anchor of CBS News The Early Show. *Previously, she was an anchor and reporter for NBC Sports for ten years. Storm became the first woman to serve as the solo anchor of a network's major sports package when she hosted NBC's coverage of the NBA, and Major League Baseball, including three World Series. Storm also served as studio host for four Olympic Games. She graduated from Notre Dame with a double major in International Government and Communications. During her junior year, she was stage manager for home game Notre Dame football broadcasts. Following an internship at WNDU, the local NBC affiliate, Storm filed sports reports on the weekend during her senior year, while acting as a Big Sister to a young girl in South Bend.*

Hannah Storm (center) and friends in front of Walsh Hall on Graduation Day 1983.

"Do not be in a great hurry to achieve success."

Hubert J. Schlafly

Class of 1941

It was quite an honor to be accepted in the undergraduate program at Notre Dame. Nineteen thirty-seven was in the height of the Great Depression, so the $1,000 a year for tuition, room and board, laundry, lab fees, and athletics was quite a strain on the family budget.

I had always been interested in photography, and when I got out to Notre Dame I found out that an undergraduate was in charge of taking the motion pictures for the athletic association. I buddied up with him, and I was appointed an official motion picture photographer for the football team. He let me do the hard work of carrying the equipment up to the stadium. When he graduated, I took over his job. For two years, I shot every game at home and also on the road, so I got to travel with the team. My salary was the largest student paid job on the campus. It was

Hubert J. Schlafly, 1941, *Dome Yearbook*.

things of that nature. My final year they started an electronics course, which was more to my liking. This excited me and became the start of my lifelong career, first with General Electric; then The Radiation Laboratory at MIT; then as director of television research at 20th Century Fox; then I was a founder, together with Irving Kahn and Fred Barton, of TelePrompTer Corporation … Other projects followed, and at the age of eighty-seven I'm still active.

Words of wisdom? Realize that you are privileged to be a member of this student body. Do not be in a great hurry to achieve success. Even as graduates, you have a lot to learn about your profession, business, and interaction with others. Welcome a variety of challenges. Each one, whether a success or failure, will contribute to your knowledge, growth, and ultimate success.

$300 a year. But the thrill of traveling the country with the football varsity was the real reward. I would have done it for free.

I had a good education at Notre Dame. I had enrolled in electrical engineering courses. At that time electrical engineering was mostly power generation or transmissions or motors and

Hubert J. Schlafly, Notre Dame Alumni Man of the Year for Fairfield County, Connecticut, in 1992, is widely known as the inventor of the TelePrompTer. During his Notre Dame days, he says, "ND was shorthand for 'No Dames.'"

"Realize that you are privileged to be a
member of this student body."

Fencers, 1940—Hubert Schlafly is third from left.

"Tear down walls of prejudice and misunder-standing."

Rabbi Albert Plotkin

Class of 1942

I grew up in South Bend, and all my cousins went to Notre Dame. I had four cousins, and we made up the Jewish student body. I wasn't sure if I should go there because it was so Catholic. And my father said, "What do you mean it's so Catholic? The Lady on top of that dome is Jewish. Don't forget it, because that's our claim to glory." Catholics and Jews are the two closest religions. We are spiritual brothers.

My best friend while I was at Notre Dame was Robert Pelton. He teaches at Notre Dame now. We roomed together because we were in the Glee Club. They put us together by names, Pelton and Plotkin. I was a secretary, who passed out the music, and they used to say of me, "Hail Mary, full of grace. Plotkin is still in first place." When I would go to bed at night, I would read my Hebrew prayers and Bob would go with his

Albert Plotkin, 1942, *Dome Yearbook*.

rosary. I thought, "Boy, this is a combination that's one of a kind."

At the same time, it was hard. My heart was very heavy; the Holocaust was beginning. We began to realize that people were being sent to concentration camps. It was a terrible time. I found faith in prayer and devotion to God. I don't think anything in history was worse than that period, especially in 1942.

While I was at Notre Dame, they didn't make me feel, because I was a Jew, that I was an outsider, especially the Glee Club. The Glee Club boys were wonderful to me. In fact, the truth of the matter is I got to be a rabbi through Notre Dame because we went to Cincinnati, and I went to Hebrew Union College for the tour. The irony of it is that I bumped into a man who was a professor. He asked me where I was from and I said South Bend. He said, "Oh my God, I was a rabbi there about forty years ago and I've always wanted a South Bend boy to get here. Are you interested?" I said yes.

Then the professor said, "Where did you get your *yeshiva*, your Hebrew training?" I replied: "Notre Dame." He said, "Well, you've got a problem." I insisted, "I got a very philosophical foundation to my religion!" and he said, "You'll be a great ecumenical boy."

So when I got there, they said, "You better watch out for Plotkin. He's a Notre Dame grad. I think he's a Vatican

"The Pope looked at me and said with his Polish accent,
'I don't think there are too many like you.'"

spy. The Pope sent him out here....You can't trust this guy. He doesn't seem so kosher!"

Later in my career, I was introduced to Pope John Paul II as a rabbi who is a Notre Dame graduate. The Pope looked at me and said with his Polish accent, "I don't think there are too many like you." I said, "Not too many. Just one."

By the way, Father Pelton was ordained to the priesthood in '49. We corresponded while we were both studying and he was moaning about all his Latin and I was moaning about all my Hebrew. We were moaning about having to learn all that stuff.

My whole life has been about building bridges. My challenge was to tear down walls of prejudice and misunderstanding. And if I can make an impact in the community in that way, then I feel like I've done a service to Jews and to Catholics.

I always felt there was a reason that I went to Notre Dame. That it would help me try to build a better world because of the tragedy of the Holocaust and the tragedy of anti-Semitism that had cursed the world. I was able to build these bridges, because I had material from both sides to cement together.

Rabbi Plotkin was the first Notre Dame graduate to become a rabbi. He graduated magna cum laude in 1942. He was the spiritual leader of Congregation Beth Israel in Arizona from 1955 to 1991. Among his many prestigious accomplishments, he was a nominee for the Dr. Thomas A. Dooley Award.

"Talent is a trust which no man has a right to ignore."

Johnny Lujack
Class of 1948

Here is something that I believe is true: Talent is a gift, but it is more than that. Talent is a trust that no man has a right to ignore. God never gave to everyone equal talent, but in His wisdom He did give to everyone the ability to make maximum use of whatever he was given.

I was ten years old and I can remember being under a radio listening to Notre Dame games. And I loved Notre Dame from that moment on. When I was a senior in high school, I was given an appointment to West Point. I said, "Well, thank you very much, but my heart's at Notre Dame. And if I can end up there, that's where I want to be." I really was not that good a high school player, but I went out to Notre Dame for a tryout and they gave me a scholar-

Opposite: Johnny Lujack (left) with Creighton Miller at a "Leahy's Lads" reunion.

"On our teams at Notre Dame, I didn't know of anyone
looking for personal honors, individual honors.
It was always about the team and winning."

ship. I kind of figured Notre Dame was going downhill if they were giving *me* a scholarship.

When I went to Notre Dame, we had four all-state quarterbacks. I was the sixth quarterback and Creighton Miller, my friend, asked, "Well, where were you all-state?" I said, "I never made all-state, but I made all-county." The next day he found out that we were the *only* high school in the county!

Creighty and I had a lot of fun together. He really was a dear friend. Maybe I missed a few days when I was at Notre Dame, but I always made it a point, right after our evening meal, to go down to the Grotto and thank the good Lord and our marvelous Mary down there for me going to Notre Dame.

I had an offer to go to Cornell. The head football coach said to me over the phone, "If you come up here to Cornell, I will pay the remaining mortgage on your mom and dad's house, I'll buy you the finest car that money can buy . . . and after you graduate from here I'll see that you get a good job." That was quite an offer. I told him, "No, I'm staying at Notre Dame." I was called into the service in 1944. When I got out of the service, rather than going home and seeing my mom and dad and family, I went to Notre Dame to be sure that I still had a scholarship. They said, "Of course you do."

Opposite: Johnny Lujack played for Notre Dame in 1943, 1946, and 1947.

Johnny Lujack, 1943.

We didn't lose a game in '46 and '47. We were the national champions in '43, '46, and '47. We really had some great returning veterans. I think anyone could have quarterbacked that team and done well. If I remember correctly, our first two teams, offense and defense, they went into pro ball, so that shows you the caliber of the people we had.

I have always felt that if you're going to be good at something, you've got to give it 100 percent. And if you want to become great at something, you got to reach down deep someplace, some way, somehow, and get another extra 10 or 20 percent. I felt that everything I tried to do at Notre Dame was with that attitude. And that is: I can do better. I think I did work a little harder. I always got out early. I was always one of the first guys out on the field and I'd get somebody to catch passes for me. Then I'd stay late and see if somebody would catch passes. That was hard to find, because they were kind of tired. I didn't have to do much work. I just had to throw the passes to them and they did all the running.

"We didn't pay much attention to anything other than practice, try to be better, and try to win the game that was coming up."

When I won the Heisman Trophy, it was the last game of the season at Southern Cal and they just told me I'd just won the Heisman. Seriously, that knocked me for a loop, because I had no idea I was in the running for the Heisman. I said, "What do I do now?" They said, "You have to go to New York." And I said, "Well, how do I get to New York?" They said, "Well, you're going to fly there." And I said, "Well, I can't fly there. I don't have any money to get there." They said, "No, they'll pay your way." And I said, "Well, what do I do?" I just absolutely didn't know. I always felt that on our teams at Notre Dame I didn't know of anyone that was looking for personal honors, individual honors. It was always about the team and winning. I think that was one of the bases for our success at Notre Dame.

We didn't pay much attention to polls and we didn't pay much attention to anything other than practice, try to be better, and try to win the game that was coming up. And that's all we tried to do. And luckily, we won them all.

Johnny Lujack won the Heisman Trophy in 1947. While at Notre Dame, he lettered in four sports (football, basketball, baseball, and track). He was inducted into The College Football Hall of Fame in 1960 and appeared on the cover of Life *magazine in 1947.*

> "Losing is a part of life, and it will only strengthen you and make you appreciate the victories more."

Regis Philbin
Class of 1953

When it came time for me to go to college, my father said, "Well, you've got go to Notre Dame." I said, "Really?" He told me that in the Marine Corps in the Pacific he met and hung around with Edward "Moose" Krause, and late at night these young officers would be around a bonfire or something out there in the jungle, and Moose would start telling them stories about Notre Dame and Knute Rockne, who he played for, and the Gipper and the Four Horsemen and all of the great legends. And these young officers were mesmerized—my father was one of them. So Moose arranged for me to go to Notre Dame. I didn't know if I could get in! My father said, "If you ever have any problems, go see Moose, by name."

I had trouble in my first semester with physics. Are you kidding me? Physics? It was required! So I went with

my physics book to see Moose! Moose said, "I love your father, but I can't help you here"—he started telling me stories about Knute Rockne again! I definitely got through physics, but that was my introduction to Moose, and I knew him all those years and loved him like we all did.

Now, unlike Hannah Storm, I didn't have the guts to go up to the radio station, knock on the door, and say, "Can I sweep the floors?" I didn't think I was talented enough. I had a big inferiority complex.

The desire was there. And I went up to the door, but I could not knock on it.

Regis Philbin, 1953, *Dome Yearbook.*

"Whenever I go back, I just inhale and I just feel so much better to see that Dome up there. It means everything to me."

So I shied away. So when it came time to pick a major, I picked sociology. It's a nice thing to rely on for the rest of your life, but it wasn't what I wanted to do.

A vivid memory of mine: When Frank Leahy came back he had been unbeaten four seasons in a row, so no one at the school when I got there in the fifth year had seen Notre Dame lose a game, and then we lost one game and people went *crazy*! They couldn't believe it— we had lost a football game! We all went around to the locker room door when they let the players hit the locker room. It was raining that day, and it was a heavy rain. We all stood in the rain waiting for Leahy to come out and explain this to us. And I remember one kid climbed a tree outside that door. It was

such a somber moment. I'll always remember it. Leahy came out and explained that we had lost and how losing is a part of life, and it will only strengthen you and make you appreciate the victories more. He was quite an inspirational speaker. I never forgot that.

I took it to heart, and then one day in 1974, I was in between jobs and running around the country and doing sports in Denver and hosting a talk show in St. Louis and I did a morning show in Chicago—this was before *Good Morning America*. I thought I was going to get that job. They kept me all summer and when it came time to decide who was going to get the job, it wasn't me. I left Chicago heartbroken.

"Whenever I go to
Notre Dame, it gives
me a warm feeling of
faith in humankind."

I couldn't go back to LA. . . . I was just heartbroken. So I drove east on the Dan Ryan Expressway and I didn't know where I was going and I wound up on the Indiana Skyway and then at the toll, the Indiana Toll Road, and I'm heading back to Notre Dame!

So I go back to Notre Dame because I thought I could rejuvenate myself. Whenever I go to Notre Dame, it gives me a warm feeling of faith in humankind. Everything that's good and decent and fair is right there on that campus—I can feel it in the air. Whenever I go back, I just inhale and I just feel so much better to see that Dome up there. It means everything to me. I drove by the stadium and there was that kid still in the tree and there was Leahy at the door and there we all were twenty-four years before, students. I went into the locker room and there was Ara Parseghian, who I had met by then, and all those great assistant coaches and they gave me some stuff to wear and I ran out, I ran around with the team. I practiced with the team. Then we timed the quarterback, and the new quarterbacks, the freshman quarterbacks coming in here, and the guy with the slowest run was Joe Montana!

So that was all part of Notre Dame. I looked at the Dome, and it rejuvenated me. I went back to LA and three months later I got a job, and I was on my way again.

Regis Francis Xavier Philbin is the Emmy Award-winning host of Live with Regis and Kelly. *He received an honorary doctor of laws degree from Notre Dame in 1999. In 2001, Regis gave Notre Dame a gift of $2.75 million, which was used to build the Regis Philbin Studio Theater.*

O'Shaughnessy Hall, 1953

"Somewhere along the way at Notre Dame was understanding the fact that your Christian faith obliges you not to just kneel down and pray, but to stand up and do."

Phil Donahue

Class of 1957

n my junior year, I got a job at WNDU. For a dollar an hour, I was an audio guy. I erased the blackboards for the weatherman. I also stood out on the small roadway with a camera pointed at me at five in the morning—I called it "doing the pigs." I was doing the farm report. I would hold the microphone and I looked into the camera and I would tell people how much barrels and hogs and pigs were on the New York Stock Exchange and the futures market. I didn't know what the hell I was talking about. There was an obligation at that time—the FCC demanded that we do something for rural audiences. I didn't realize it until a lot later in life: There were no farmers watching me. The *cameraman* wasn't even watching. But by golly, I was Phil Donahue on TV. And we were *live*. Talk about pumped.

What I remember somewhere along

the way at Notre Dame was understanding the fact that your Christian faith obliges you not to just kneel down and pray, but to stand up and do. We had a very good theology teacher at Notre Dame, Father James P. Smyth. It was exciting—this was a guy that wanted us to think for ourselves. And who wanted us to be challenged. I'll

Above: Phil Donahue, 1957, *Dome Yearbook*. Opposite: Phil Donahue with an audience member of his daytime talk show *Donahue*, which ran from 1974 to 1996.

never forget him. He really broke the mold of "Who made me? God made me," the whole catechism memory thing. I began to ask more and more questions. I had fewer and fewer answers, but it was much more exciting. I really thank him. Because then suddenly I had a show where I got paid for answering and asking questions. We were making enough noise that some very important people were coming on, like senators and congressmen. They wanted the exposure. Then we put on gay people and got a really great reputation with the politically active gay community. I'm very proud to say I was the first GLAAD Media Awards recipient. I have people come up to me to this day saying, "Thank you, Mr. Donahue. Because of you, I came out to my parents." And women saying, "Thank you, Mr. Donahue, because of you I got out of an abusive marriage."

I once interviewed Linus Pauling. He's won two Nobel Prizes, chemistry and peace. He said to me, "You can't have good ideas unless you have a lot of them." I always liked that. Another one is Tennyson, listen to this: "There lives

"Question authority—it's a wonderful, virtuous, patriotic, American thing to do."

more faith in honest doubt, believe me, than in half the creeds." That takes my breath away. Tennyson speaks to me. What he essentially does is encourage people not to be crushed by doubt, but to see it as natural. It's a sign of, and this is just my opinion, having a wonderful brain that God gave you, that He obliges you to exercise, to use, to question, to make things better, to not accept. To think for yourself.

And we were raised in the fifties, when parents used to say, "If they didn't know what they were talking about, they wouldn't be in Washington." Then years later, I interviewed Noam Chomsky. I said, "What are you trying to say?" He said, "Never ever trust the state." I was like, "What do you mean, never trust the state?" I was brought up to believe that America is always good. Dissent was not encouraged in my childhood. We weren't really sharpened to the point of understanding the democracy. But that's what we should be proud of. We don't have to march blindly. Question authority—it's a wonderful, virtuous, patriotic, American thing to do.

Phil Donahue, widely credited for inventing the talk show platform, debuted The Phil Donahue Show *in 1967 and from 1974 to 1996 hosted the acclaimed show* Donahue. *He has won nineteen Emmy Awards. While at Notre Dame, he played Biff in* Death of a Salesman.

Opposite: Phil Donahue (right) as Lt. Stephen Maryk in *The Caine Mutiny Court-Martial* at University of Notre Dame (1956).

> "The Notre Dame experience is something you'll carry through life. Don't waste it."

John McMeel

Class of 1957

Notre Dame was an ongoing experience for me in my family. I mean, we were just *consumed* with Notre Dame. We used to turn toward the Golden Dome and we said our blessing before meals. And my dad was the university doctor as well as the team doctor. Rockne got him that job in 1931, but I was on the sidelines with Dad when I was only about nine years old. I'll never forget Johnny Lujack putting his hand on my head. That was something. I said I'd never wash my hair for months!

Being a student there was one thing, but Notre Dame was a way of life with us. We had lost Studebaker. We had lost Singer Manufacturing Company. All over South Bend we were going through some tough times, but we always had Notre Dame. That was, you know, something you consumed even as a teenager because I knew where I

"It's those people who made up the university who made
such an imprint on me, and it was glorious."

was going. There wasn't going to be any
Indiana State or Purdue or anyplace
else like that in my future. There was
only Notre Dame. It was the only school
I applied to. I had to hold my breath because my grades weren't the best. I got
in "on condition" for a semester. I was
planning to live on campus, but my
father passed away my junior year in
high school, so I stayed at home with
Mother.

I'll never forget that: just the experience from that semester, saying, "God,
I gotta make it. I gotta cut it." And it
happened.

John McMeel, 1957, *Dome Yearbook*.

Accounting wasn't my bag—that's when I wondered whether I made the right choice as far as business school was concerned. I had a guy named Slowey that got me through. The students there, my classmates, were from all walks of life and they weren't all rich, which was good because we weren't either.

There was an experience there. It was the caliber of the person not only academically. I mean, Notre Dame was good, but not where it is today. The Notre Dame experience is something you'll carry through life. Don't waste it. It was the individuals, and our class has shown that very, very much because we stay so closely in contact, especially now with the Internet. It's those people who made up the university who made such an imprint on me, and it was glorious.

John McMeel is chairman and president of Andrews McMeel Universal, the largest independent newspaper syndicate in the world. As a "townie," he was one of the few car owners on campus, a privilege he used to his advantage, earning him the nickname "Deals."

"In glorious victory or agonizing defeat, carry yourself with dignity."

Tommy Hawkins

Class of 1959

I have been blessed with success and have traveled all over the world, but my four years at Notre Dame have been the best time of my life. It was there I became a man and I prepared myself to meet the challenges of the world.

My all-time favorite sports memory happened in 1958 at the old Chicago Stadium. There were twenty thousand standing-room-only fans on hand for a Saturday-night college doubleheader featuring Loyola of Chicago against Kentucky, and Notre Dame battling defending national champion North Carolina. With no starting player over six feet five inches tall, we were one of the smallest teams in the country.

In the first game, Loyola shocked Kentucky by defeating the Wildcats on a last-second, half-court hook shot by Art McZier. That electrified the overflow

"I was taught you can blend your personal energy
with that of others, thereby creating a synergistic force
that can far surpass individual energy."

crowd and set the stage for our magic moment, our victorious finale.

I was a Chicago native and that year's Chicago Stadium college player of the year, so the victory over North Carolina may have been my finest hour and one of Notre Dame's all-time basketball greatest hits.

My basketball coaches were Johnny Jordan and Jim Gibbons, both former Irish players, both super role models. They took a proprietary interest in me as an athlete, a student, and a develop-

Opposite: Tommy Hawkins receiving his B.A. degree from Father Hesburgh, 1959.

ing social being. Far above the success we achieved on the basketball court was their insistence that I be respected as a quality student, and that I develop my personal and social skills. And I learned: In glorious victory or agonizing defeat, carry yourself with dignity. It was Jordan who taught me to be a public speaker. He took me with him to his speaking engagements, starting me off with short two-minute presentations. As I developed, he increased my time at the podium. Jordan also insisted I take public speaking and elocution classes. By the time I was a senior, I was flying around the country speaking on behalf

"With no starting player over six feet five inches tall, we were one of the smallest teams in the country."

of the University. To this day, I make a minimum of fifty presentations a year.

At Notre Dame I was taught you can blend your personal energy with that of others, thereby creating a synergistic force that can far surpass individual energy. This invaluable lesson has projected me in so many directions and helped me to achieve success that I never dreamed possible.

Tommy Hawkins recently retired from his eighteen-year career with the Los Angeles Dodgers, where he was vice president of communications, then external affairs. He currently heads his own public relations firm in Santa Monica, Hawkins Communications, Inc. In June 1999, Hawkins received the Sorin Award, which is given annually to an outstanding Notre Dame alumnus.

Opposite: Tommy Hawkins, 1959, *Dome Yearbook*.

"There is always someone to remind you of what is essential."

Reverend Edward A. Malloy, C.S.C.

Class of 1963

Notre Dame was the place where I was able to test out my capacities in a number of leadership positions. After I ran for senior class president and lost, I served during my senior year as president of Badin Hall. It was a great chance to come to know all the members of the dorm and to try to be responsible for maximizing our sense of community.

In another role as an elected member of the Blue Circle Honor Society, I came to know a broad cross section of my fellow students in a fun-filled and service-oriented way. As a member of the Notre Dame basketball team, I learned firsthand the significance of the phrase "the thrill of victory, the agony of defeat."

I never imagined when I was a student that I would return not only to join the Notre Dame faculty as a

member of the theology department but later to serve in various levels of administration. My life as a teacher and scholar has always been a great joy. To watch young people grow up before your very eyes and to have them share their hopes and dreams as well as their failures and disappointments is a special privilege. To live in a dorm as long as I have, for so many years, provided another occasion to interact with students on a personal level.

My eighteen years as president allowed me to meet Notre Dame people around the country and throughout the world. Their manifest sense of pride about the university and their desire for it to maintain its distinctiveness as a Catholic university was a source of inspiration for me. Even on those occasions when things did not go as smoothly as I hoped. There is always someone around to remind you of what is essential.

Men's basketball team with Edward A. Malloy (top row, left), 1961, *Dome Yearbook.*

Nothing has given me more pleasure in my years at Notre Dame than the opportunity to celebrate the Eucharist in dorm chapels, in the Basilica of the Sacred Heart, in the Joyce Center, and in other settings around the campus. For me as a Catholic Christian, the Eucharist is at the center of things. It is the most vivid and concrete sacramental way that we have to unite ourselves with Jesus the Lord and to be reinforced in our sense of faith by the presence of others who share common convictions with us. On no occasion was all of this more evident to me than on the after-

Edward A. Malloy, 1963, *Dome Yearbook.*

"To watch young people grow up before your very eyes and to have them share their hopes and dreams as well as their failures and disappointments is a special privilege."

noon of September 11, 2001, when thousands and thousands of Notre Dame people gathered for mass on the South Quad to seek consolation and strength in the wake of the horrible attacks on the East Coast.

Notre Dame is far from a perfect institution. But few places have the power to evoke such passion, such pride, and such a sense of being a part of something larger than ourselves. My hope and prayer is that this mystique, this special sense, might captivate subsequent generations of students and friends in the same way that it has been an integral part of my life since 1959.

Reverend Edward "Monk" Malloy, C.S.C., served as the sixteenth president of Notre Dame, from 1987 to 2005. During his presidency, Notre Dame's operating budget and research-funding endowments grew exponentially, the library more than doubled in size, endowed-chair holders quadrupled, and women came to make up nearly half the student body. While attending Notre Dame, he was a one-year varsity letterman (basketball), and he continued to play Bookstore Basketball throughout most of his presidency.

Above: Dining hall, 1960s. Opposite: Students in Hurley Hall, 1960s.

"In life, you have to take risks … the road less traveled."

Matthew V. Storin

Class of 1964

I attended Notre Dame during its blackest days as a football power—the 1960–63 seasons. Only two classes in Notre Dame history went through its four years without at least one winning season—mine and the class before mine (which included our former president, Father Malloy). I was head football manager for the '63 season under interim head coach Hugh Devore. I am way overinvested in Notre Dame football, perhaps because of all those losing seasons during my student days. As a manager, I made six road trips without a single victory! My greatest moment in connection with Notre Dame football actually came in 2002. I made the trip with the team to play Air Force. We won the game, 21–14, and came back to South Bend with a 7–0 record. When the buses pulled onto Juniper Road about 4 A.M. and I saw that lighted Dome, I had a feeling that

wiped away a lot of that frustration from long ago.

What I learned, however, were lessons of loyalty. We still had a core of die-hard fans who met on road trips, took us (managers, not the team, of course) to dinner, and invited us to their homes. At a time like right now, it is easy to find people who worship Notre Dame football, but I always remembered—some by name—the people who were loyal to us in the dark days.

I took a risk in going to Notre Dame. I grew up in western Massachusetts, a

Matthew V. Storin, 1964, *Dome Yearbook*.

"I always remembered—some by name—the people
who were loyal to us in the dark days."

long way from South Bend. At my high school, the smart kids were expected to go to Holy Cross or, if they were truly adventuresome, Boston College. Travel in those days was less accessible than it is today. If you went that far to school, you didn't generally come home for Thanksgiving or at semester break. I chose to go to Notre Dame partly because it was, from my particular part of the world, the road less traveled. That decision has always been part of my Notre Dame experience. Even today, with my coming back to work at Notre Dame, my East Coast friends are a bit incredulous that anyone would willingly live in the Midwest. In life, you have to take risks—not of physical danger necessarily but the road less traveled.

Matthew V. Storin is an adjunct professor in the Department of American Studies at Notre Dame. He is the former editor of The Boston Globe, *which won four Pulitzer Prizes under his direction. He gets together every year with his friends from the fourth floor of Walsh Hall.*

"All anyone needs is a start."

Bill Dwyre
Class of 1966

It was my junior year, 1964–65. My roommate and I had a plan. We would hit the world of sports media like a tornado.

All we needed, all anyone needs, was a start.

My roommate's name was George Blaha, and, like so many of us at Notre Dame in the mid-1960s, sports was our world. Yes, we went to class and did our best. But we had to. Yes, we were crazy about females, but shyness and general inaccessibility kept much of that drive in check.

So the outlet, the reason for getting out of bed every morning, was sports.

The Blaha-Dwyre plan was simple: cut a few audition tapes of our play-by-play work, send them to all the area radio stations that carried high school football games, and offer our services.

The fee was going to be workable

for all the stations. We would work for free.

It never occurred to us that there would be any hesitation. We discussed how to choose among stations when the phone calls started pouring in. The best solution seemed to be: take the first offer.

Blaha was to be the play-by-play per-son. He was glib, hip, knowledgeable, and—most important—more worldly than I. He had lived in two states, Iowa and Michigan, before arriving in South Bend. Plus, he had practiced. While others sang in the shower, Blaha did play-by-play: "Jay Miller, the pride of Indiana state basketball, drives the lane, floats in the air like a bird, and dishes to Walt Sahm. He banks it in and the Irish lead!"

I was more the word guy, a communication arts major with an eye on newspapers. But the world of sports radio was fascinating, and listeners certainly would overlook my less-than-deep tones and quirky Wisconsin accent once they discovered the marvels of my color analysis.

And so the tapes went out and the wait began. Days, then weeks passed, and crushed egos awoke each day to the dread of more gloom.

Then it arrived in the mail. It was a letter from a well-known South Bend broadcaster named Frank Crosiar, who not only did lots of play-by-play of local events but also handled the public-address duties at Notre Dame football games.

Bill Dwyre, 1966, *Dome Yearbook*.

"Crosiar suggested that we both think of getting out of the media business now, while we were young, because he didn't think either of us had much future."

The letter was opened eagerly. The contents were taken with stunned silence. In essence, Crosiar had told us he listened, didn't think much of what he heard, and suggested that we both think of getting out of the media business now, while we were young, because he didn't think either of us had much future.

So we did no high school play-by-play, for free or otherwise. Eventually we went our separate ways, Blaha getting a master's degree in Business Administration at the University of Michigan and then pursuing his life love at some little ten-watt radio station in Adrian, Michigan. I headed for the newspaper business.

Flash-forward twenty years or so.

Blaha comes to Los Angeles as the veteran voice of the Detroit Pistons. He calls his college friend, Bill Dwyre, now the longtime sports editor of the *Los Angeles Times,* to be his halftime guest.

Somewhere during the interview, the Frank Crosiar story is told and everybody gets a big laugh.

A few days later, Dwyre gets a letter from somebody who had been listening that night back in Detroit. The letter is short, to the point. It says: "Heard you and Blaha on the Pistons game the other night. Frank Crosiar was right."

George Blaha is among the deans of NBA broadcasters, and is now in his thirtieth year with the Pistons.

Bill Dwyre has been sports editor of the Los Angeles Times *for twenty-five years. Among many other awards, he was named Editor of the Year by the National Press Foundation in 1984. At Notre Dame he was a Communication Arts major.*

"Make yourself vulnerable: The rewards far outweigh the risk of getting hurt."

Joseph Kernan

Class of 1968

My attitude has always been and remains today that I'm better because of the people I know and the friends that I have and the people that I've had a chance to work with. My father and his father before him always said, "You're only as good as your ball club." And I believe that to be true.

When I look back on my time at Notre Dame, I think about the friendships that I formed. For me, that was the great value that I got out of Notre Dame. After I got shot down as a naval flight officer during the Vietnam War, the first guy that I made contact with informed me that our escort had lost us and we were presumed killed. I had visions of my family and what they were going through. It was one of the worst days of my life. It was three months later when I got a package

Joseph Kernan, 1968, *Dome Yearbook*.

from home, or I was told it was from home, but I knew that they could just throw stuff in a box and tell me that my family had sent me something. But I needed some sign, something that would be proof to me, that my family knew that I was alive. In the package there were, among other things, three handkerchiefs. I looked at the first one, then the second one, and down in the corner of the third handkerchief was printed in ink: "These are compliments of Sammy and Wheels." Sammy and Wheels were nicknames for two friends I went to school with and who were at the time just getting back home from Vietnam. And I knew then that not only my family knew I was alive, but my friends from Notre Dame were there

"I'm better because of the people I know and the friends that I have and the people that I've had a chance to work with."

with my family and helping them through it.

It was literally one of the best days of my life, because I knew then that my family knew that I was okay and obviously still thought I had my sense of humor. But it's one of those things that's indicative of the kinds of friends that I made in school and the kinds of friends that I still have today.

If you want to be successful and you want to have fun, you really can only do that with other people. I think you have to be open to that possibility. For some people, that's hard. It's hard to open yourself up, to make yourself vulnerable, but the rewards far outweigh the risk of getting hurt somehow.

Joseph Kernan is the former governor of Indiana. He has also served as lieutenant governor of Indiana and mayor of South Bend. He twice received Purple Hearts while serving as a naval flight officer. He played baseball all four years at Notre Dame, but says he had to give up his dream to play second base for the Chicago White Sox because he never could hit a curveball.

"Work as a team."

Terry Hanratty

Class of 1969

We grew up poor but we didn't know it. If we wanted to have a basketball game, you just yelled out the back door and you had fifteen kids in your backyard. It's so different from today's society. My mother was forty-one years old when she had me. She was five foot four and about a hundred pounds, and I was a ten-pound-plus baby. I was delivered by my Italian grandmother. The doctor showed up an hour after I was born to check me out, and he wrote a bill for five bucks. My grandmother tore it up and in her best English told him *she* did all the work. She wouldn't pay five bucks for me to come into the world. Frugal! Frugal, we called her!

I think at age seventeen, I made the best decision of my life—to go to Notre

Opposite: Terry Hanratty coaching his son's team, the New Canaan Red football team.

Dame. They were the only school that promised me nothing but the opportunity to play quarterback. Most schools would tell me that you couldn't play as a freshman. You had to start as a sophomore. Or if you don't start as a sophomore, you're going to start as wide receiver. I said, "Whoa, not me!" To this day, I can remember sitting down with Ara Parseghian. We ate at the Pittsburgh Hilton hotel, in the little coffee shop there. Looking at the menu, I saw "steak sandwich," which was like $4.95. I remember thinking that if I get that, Ara will think I'm gouging him. So I went for the club sandwich, which was like $2.95. I spent two hours with Ara, and it was a done deal. He was so trusting and so sincere that you knew, talking to him, that this was going to be your father figure for the next four years.

It was a little overwhelming because first of all, there were no women there, which I was not accustomed to, but a

**Terry Hanratty, playing against
Northwestern, 1968.**

"I got out of there thinking I had played the worst game ever."

good point was that you could wear the same clothes for a month. There's no one there to impress.

So Sunday nights, every week, you'd have your meal and you watch Saturday's game on tape. I was in there cocky as can be because at Saturday's game I'd had three touchdown passes and threw for over three hundred yards, ran the ball well, no interceptions. All of a sudden, the lights went out. The projectors went on and from the first play, they chewed me out: "Look at that footwork here. That's just horrible. He was wide open. You should have thrown to him first." I got out of there thinking I had played the worst game ever, but Ara's smart. Here he had this senior team with two potential *pains*: the quarterback and the wide receiver. He must have thought, "I'm popping their legs out from under them real quick." I walked out of that meeting and erased that *I* out of *team* and put that *e* back in.

So we were ingrained to do that. My coaching philosophy now—I coach my kids' teams—is work as a team, especially with football, because it's the ultimate team sport.

Terry Hanratty was a three-year starter for the Irish as quarterback in 1966–68 and a consensus All-America pick in 1968. He played with Pittsburgh from 1969 to 1975 and Tampa Bay in 1976. Before his first big game against Purdue at Notre Dame, while his teammates were too nervous to eat, he had steak, eggs, and a baked potato for breakfast.

Opposite: Stadium, 1970s.

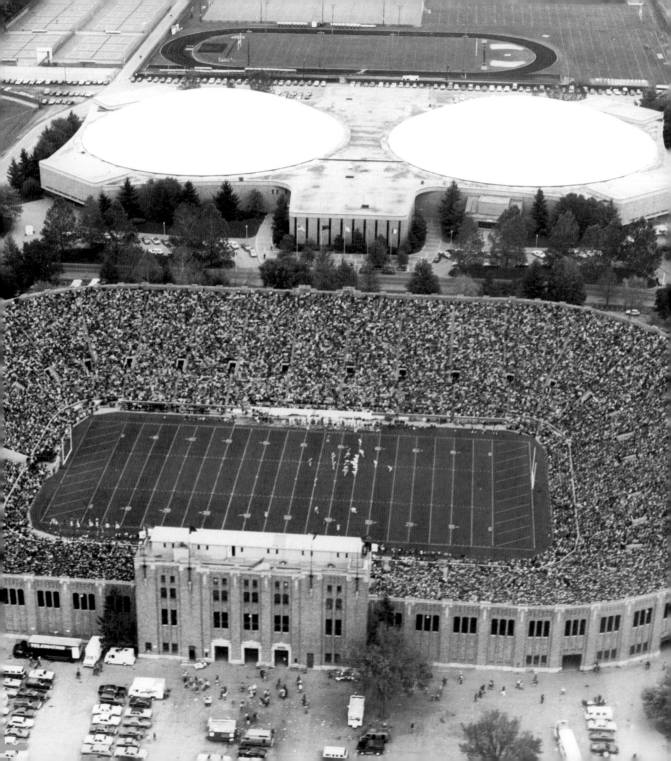

"The idea is
to give the
knowledge
and wisdom
learned at
Notre Dame
to others."

Dr. Dennis M. Nigro
Class of 1969

I was born into living the Notre Dame life. Within the next several years, my family will have gone to school there for over a hundred years. My grandfather was a very good friend and classmate of Knute Rockne. He brought Rockne to South Bend, and after Rockne's death, helped raise his children. So the spirit of "God, Country, Notre Dame" has always been a part of my life.

The spiritual awakening that I believe I received was a result of listening to some tapes of Dr. Thomas Dooley when I was on a high school retreat at Rockhurst High School. His words of service as well as his letter to Father Hesburgh, as Dr. Dooley lay dying, provoked an ideal in me. I spent the next four decades carrying it out.

Also serving as a catalyst for me was when, several months before I gradu-

> "Sometimes to get through life, you have to have a different way of looking at things."

Jimmy Brogan

Class of 1970

Most of the stuff I use in my career as a comedian I learned outside the classroom, like I partnered with Bill Eiler ['72] on a radio show at WSND, and I hosted an impression contest for An Tostal weekend (loosely translated, it means festival, or merrymaking).

This was an alternative weekend to the big formal prom weekend. It consisted of bed races, pie-eating contests, capturing pigs in a mud pit, and, in its fifth year, the Bookstore Basketball Tournament. It was during the An Tostal impersonation contest that I made my first ad lib on stage.

I had a friend in Carroll Hall named Mark Tracy who did an impression of Ed Sullivan. It always made me laugh. When I was at a meeting of the An Tostal spring weekend committee I suggested we hold an impersonation con-

test. I figured if Mark could do an impression, there must be more kids on campus who do impressions. I had envisioned a few people standing under a tree doing impressions and then some sort of ribbon as a prize. When they asked who would run it, I volunteered.

We decided to hold the contest on the South Quad right in front of Alumni Hall. When the day arrived, the committee had somehow gotten ahold of a four-foot-tall portable stage and a huge speaker system. And there were five hundred students sitting on the lawn waiting for the contest. I was scared to death, but I had told the committee I would emcee the event and they held me to my word.

About halfway through the event, Father Hesburgh walked by—a rare sighting in those days. I pointed him out and he waved to the crowd. As the ovation quieted down, I said, "Actually, that is not Father Hesburgh, it's Father Joyce doing an impression of Father Hesburgh." I realize that it is not the

Opposite: Jimmy Brogan, manning a concession stand before a football game, 1970.

> "As the ovation quieted down, I said, 'Actually, that is not Father Hesburgh, it's Father Joyce doing an impression of Father Hesburgh.' "

funniest ad lib of all time—far from it, actually—but it was in the moment and quite a departure from the stilted introductions that I was reading off cards and the stolen impressions I was attempting onstage. It was off the top of my head, it was original, and it got a laugh. This set me on the path to thinking that I could actually try stand-up comedy. With all this experience, how could I fail?

Well, quite easily, it turned out. My first time onstage in New York City was at a club called Catch a Rising Star. I did an impression of my old friend and now legendary rector of Keenan Hall, Father Robert Griffin. What was amus-

"After all, I was an expert at comedy. I had once gotten a laugh on an ad lib at Notre Dame."

ing to a few people at Notre Dame get-togethers was completely lost on the hard-bitten New York City crowd. Plus of course they had no idea who he was. The impression could have been dead on and still they would have been puzzled. But I was so sure they were wrong that the next night I tried it again at another club. After all, I was an expert at comedy. I had once gotten a laugh on an ad lib at Notre Dame.

Same result. The emcee, coming back to the stage to stunned silence, could think of nothing positive to say. All he could think of was, "That's the tallest white comedian I've ever seen." Sure, that might not have been the biggest compliment—in fact, he was actually making fun of me, and that might have crushed some people, but not me. He actually called me a "come-dian." I had arrived. Minutes before, I wasn't even a comedian.

Sometimes to get though life, you have to have a different way of looking at things.

Jimmy Brogan is a comedian who has appeared on The Tonight Show Starring Johnny Carson *and* Late Night with David Letterman. *He hosted* Laffathon *(Showtime),* Comic Strip Live *(Fox), and* You Asked for It, Again *(Family Channel). For nearly a decade he helped create Jay Leno's* Tonight Show *monologues. At Notre Dame he wrote humorous pieces for the campus paper* The Observer.

Opposite: Student Senate—Jimmy Brogan is in the top row, second from left, 1970.

"To love God and to reverence God is the secret of finding yourself."

Most Reverend Daniel R. Jenky, C.S.C., D.D.

Class of 1970

'm a Holy Cross religious and I love Notre Dame, but clearly what makes Notre Dame special is faith and God. That understanding you get that God is God and we are not. To love God and to reverence God is the secret of finding yourself. Everything that we do for everybody else is, I think, what happens when we realize that it's not words in a book. You realize that God loves you. If there is ever a place, except maybe the Vatican, where our Catholic faith is so manifest, it is at Notre Dame. And that's what captured me and got me through calculus and the ups and downs and finding my vocation. I have to say, as a dorm priest, you did have many opportunities to have conversations with students about God, and about their life, and about finding themselves. I had never planned on being a bishop, for sure; I still think I

got an RA to go and get him and bring
him back to my room. He assumed he
was about to be killed for a keg of beer.
We had to make arrangements to drive
him to Chicago. Someone was with him
all the time up until when we were
supposed to leave. But at some point,
we lost him—we could not find him.

And we had deliberately planned to
have someone with him all the time,
because suicide is a tough thing with
adolescents—it can be contagious. So
we raced all around campus looking for
him. And where did we find him? At the
Grotto. And this is not a guy who necessarily was at mass every Sunday. There
he was, very naturally praying at the
Grotto in his great grief. So I do think

Daniel R. Jenky, 1970, *Dome Yearbook.*

"Notre Dame allows people to experience their eternal values, their spirituality."

Notre Dame allows people to experience their eternal values, their spirituality. I wouldn't even be ashamed to say it: Emotional Catholic Christianity is all there. And it works.

I've seen that so often. Guys that I used to yell at to get the beer out of the hallway, they're now with their kids lighting candles at mass. It's deeply moving to me. If I live to seventy-five, I will be the cantankerous old bishop on the front porch at Corby Hall. It's not at all unusual to have somebody say, "I just flew in from Los Angeles. It's been thirty years." I mean, they literally just come back there for important moments in their life. It's a powerful place for our faith.

I'll draw on Notre Dame all my life, if God will allow me to retire there. When I'm doing confirmations in Kickapoo, Illinois, I'm still drawing on what I have learned at Notre Dame.

Most Reverend Daniel R. Jenky, C.S.C., D.D., is Bishop of Peoria. While he was studying at Notre Dame he used to go on midnight excursions to rescue old art and religious artifacts from the attics of various campus buildings and return them to the Basilica; one time he and his fellow priests were stopped by security—at 3:30 A.M.!

"There is more than one way to answer a question."

Rabbi Richard Libowitz

Class of 1970

I am a Jew who attended the best-known Catholic university in the world. I did so, in part, because it was so different from what I had known. I was a liberal Jewish kid from Connecticut, attending a somewhat conservative Catholic school in the Midwest. I knew college had to be more than classes, and I thought it was important to learn about people who were unlike me. I had questions, and people had many questions for me about my faith, questions that I couldn't always answer.

I was not a regular synagogue attendee at home, but I attended many a Friday-evening service while in South Bend, because a classmate or Saint Mary's friend had always wanted to see a Jewish service, and would I take them? Their questions forced me to think about my answers.

In those years of political and social turmoil [1966–1970], I saw many of my

"In those years of political and social turmoil, I saw many of my classmates struggling with their faith."

classmates struggling with their faith, asking how, as Catholics, they should react to the war in Vietnam. Many, at the time, stopped calling themselves Catholic and used the term *Christian,* and many war protests were shaped with religious arguments and symbolism. After four years at Notre Dame, I wanted to know what it meant to be me, and about six weeks after graduation I began a year of study in Israel, which led me next to rabbinical school and graduate study in Religion. So in large part, I owe my becoming a rabbi to my Notre Dame experience.

While at Notre Dame, I was fortunate to have many fine teachers. One who stands out as a mentor is Willis Nutting, who was a true Renaissance figure. I took a Theology course and a Collegiate Seminar class with him and even went on one of his 5 A.M. nature expeditions. He enjoyed the classroom, was never upset by a student's statements, and was infinitely patient, no matter how far class discussion diverged from the scheduled topic. He once asked a question which I have repeated to my students to this present day: "How far are we from the nearest desert?" People thought of the Mojave, the Sahara, and our guesses measured thousands of miles. "Twelve inches," he said. "Remove the top twelve inches of soil and nothing will grow here. And a place where nothing will grow is a desert." That different sense of perspective taught me a valuable lesson: that there is more than one way to answer a question.

Rabbi Richard Libowitz is lecturer in the Intellectual Heritage Program at Temple University and an adjunct member of the Theology Department of Saint Joseph's University. He is the author or editor of nine books, including The Genocidal Mind *(Paragon House, 2005). While he attended Notre Dame he was one of three Jewish students.*

Richard Libowitz (bearded) and Pat McDonough, senior year, spring of 1970, prepping for the Boston Marathon (though neither man ran in Boston, Libowitz did subsequently run in other marathons).

Above: Students on campus, 1974. Opposite: Students on campus, circa 1970s.

"Never let anyone tell you that you cannot do something."

Joe Theismann

Class of 1971

I was one of thirteen quarterbacks that were recruited in 1967. Back then, the way the university recruited was they would try to recruit the best athletes and then from that class of thirteen, two would go on to become wide receivers, two would go on to become linebackers, three would go on to become defensive backs. So you had a core of athletes. Not necessarily like it is today, where you recruit specifically to the position, but you had a core of athletes that were just good enough to play in different places. Of course, Notre Dame had won the national championship, beating USC, the previous year. I was a part of a freshman class at the university and I was just quite awed by the guys from the year before. I was about to join a national champion football team.

I returned punts my first seven games. We played one game my fresh-

"I told him it was Thees-mann.
He said, 'No, it's not. It's THIGHS-mann.' "

man year. We used to have the varsity beat us up. That was our purpose: to be beat up by the varsity team. We were just somebody that they could just kill, fresh meat, without killing each other. And that was our purpose in life. My sophomore year, I wound up playing the last three games after Terry Hanratty got hurt. The beginning of my senior year is when Roger Valdisseri, during spring practice, was standing on the sidelines with a reporter on the *Chicago Tribune*. Roger was the sports information director. He's standing on the sidelines talking about me, and the reporter said, "Is that Theismann as in Heisman out there?"

I guess Roger got that in his mind and called me into his office and asked me how I pronounced my last name. I told him it was "Thees-mann." He said, "No, it's not. It's 'THIGHS-mann.' " I called my grandmother, who's sort of the patron saint of our family. I said, "Granny, look, they want to change the pronunciation of our last name." She said, "What? What?" I said, "To Thighs-mann." It turns out that's how our name was originally pronounced. So she said, "That's fine with me." So I got the blessing from my grandmother and our name was changed. Obviously, there was the big "Theismann for Heisman" and all that kind of stuff. And today I am Joe Theismann. It's one

Opposite: Theismann and Parseghian, 1969.

of the great impacts that the university had on my life.

I entered college at about 150 pounds. And after I made the decision to go to Notre Dame, there was an article in a local Jersey paper. Basically the headline said something like: "Theismann will get killed at Notre Dame." That had always sort of been my battle cry: Never let anyone tell you that you cannot do something. That's been my life story. I've always been too small. I've always been too short. They would say, "Scrambling quarterbacks can't win Super Bowls." And "Your arm's not strong enough." Actually, when I walked off the plane at the University of Notre Dame, Joe Yonto was our defensive line coach and he was the gentleman who had recruited me. There was a linebacker coach by the name of Johnny Ray who was standing there with Joe, and Joe was talking about this terrific young quarterback coming from New Jersey. I step off the plane and Johnny Ray looks at Joe Yonto and says, "Where is he? Where's this football player?" He said, "He's right there." He said, "My God, he doesn't look like he could carry the water bucket, much less quarterback a football."

All along the way, everybody always tried to tell me that there were facets of my life or my abilities that would inhibit me from achieving ultimate goals that I wanted. All that did was motivate me.

Joe Theismann led the Fighting Irish to consecutive Cotton Bowls and was runner-up to Jim Plunkett in the Heisman Trophy balloting in 1970. His professional football career began with the Toronto Argonauts of the Canadian Football League (after being drafted by the Miami Dolphins and Major League Baseball's Minnesota Twins) and flourished with the Washington Redskins, culminating with a victory in Super Bowl XVII. He is currently an analyst for ESPN's Monday Night Football.

Opposite: Joe Theismann played for Notre Dame from 1967 to 1971.

"Share the excitement and wonder of learning and opportunity with others."

Marc Maurer

Class of 1974

Whent I enrolled at Notre Dame I was then, as I am now, totally blind. I had received training in the skills of blindness: how to travel with a cane, how to communicate using the typewriter, how to read and write Braille, and the like. However, my training had occurred in Des Moines, Iowa, a city laid out with blocks divided by streets. When I got to the campus, it had almost no streets. Many paths crossed the campus, and some of them seemed to proceed in straight lines. The layout seemed bewildering.

Then there was the problem of where to get lunch. What was the way to the dining hall, and what were the procedures involved in getting the food?

When I had been in high school, I wondered what my life would become.

At the age of sixteen, my fellow students got driver's licenses and jobs. I was unable to get a driver's license, and nobody seemed to want me for work. Consequently, I thought that education must be my passport to a productive life. When I got the notice of acceptance from Notre Dame, it seemed to be a tremendous opportunity and an enormous challenge. I was delighted and very apprehensive.

Blind people who travel with a cane identify their location very much as sighted people do it—we look for landmarks that give us some idea of where we are, what direction we are heading, and what else is nearby. I had learned to travel using streets as primary markers of my path of progress. On the new campus streets were rare, and I needed to find other markers to identify my location and the path for getting where I wanted to go. The buildings on the campus have names, but the paths between them do not. However, by asking dozens of questions, I got the terrain laid out in my head with sufficient clarity so that I could find my way.

Then there were problems of how to get the books, how to find people prepared to read them to me, and how to read everything else, such as handouts from professors in class. Dr. Emil T. Hoffman taught chemistry. He provided a weekly recording of a study guide on cassette tape. I may have been the most

Marc Maurer, 1974, *Dome Yearbook*.

"I found that almost universally there was an openness to experimenting with ways for me to learn."

grateful freshman chemistry student on campus.

Everybody at Notre Dame takes gym class. This I learned during the first week. But the coaches didn't seem to know what to do with me. When we talked about the need for physical training, they said that they would waive the class for me. But I didn't want to do that. I wanted to be a part of the whole experience, and I urged that I be accepted among the others. They asked me what I could do, and we considered the matter. Eventually, we settled on ice skating. I had never before worn a pair of skates, but by the end of the semester I was able to take to the ice without tumbling onto it and with joy in the feeling of the moment.

At the university neither I nor my teachers knew for certain what would be expected of me, but I found that almost universally there was an openness to experimenting with ways for me to learn. I came to understand that my participation could be complete and that I could shape the talent latent within me and use it to share the excitement and wonder of learning and opportunity with others.

Marc Maurer, J.D., is president of the National Federation of the Blind. Though he began Notre Dame as an engineering major, he graduated cum laude from the Great Books Program.

> "Be open to meeting new and different people.... Do not cling to all the values and people that you have just spent your whole life with."

Honorable Ann Claire Williams

Class of 1975

I came to Notre Dame for law school in 1972, which was the first year undergraduate women came to campus. When I was a second-year law student, I became assistant rector of Farley Hall. There are a variety of kinds of people that can be rectors: sometimes religious, sometimes professors who are single, and often the assistant rectors are graduate students, like myself.

Farley had previously been an all-male hall. It was interesting when we opened the hall and many of the girls came in with their fathers who were saying, "This was *my* dorm." The rector of Farley Hall was Sister Jean Lenz, and it was her first year at Notre Dame, and we didn't know each other—we were each hired independently.

I had gone to Catholic high school, so I only knew nuns as instructors. Even though I had close relationships with

"I felt like I was a part of that spirit and participated in groundbreaking history for women."

some of the nuns, this was a very different experience to relate as a peer—we had to run this hall together. I wasn't a person that stereotyped, especially in the position that I'm in as an African American, but I did have a more formal, traditional view of nuns. I didn't know whether I would be getting a holier-than-thou type or if she'd be a real person. Sister Jean Lenz is very down-to-earth, very easygoing, very easy to deal with. And although she's deeply religious, she's not one of those people to wear her religion on her sleeve. And she was a real person, so the experience of getting to know her did give me more insight into the religious life and how real her mission was.

It was very exciting opening the dorm to women that year. We felt like we were part of history. As I said, we didn't know each other, and after about a week of weathering the storm, getting all these kids moved in, it was very exciting and we were both new to this.

Sister Jean Lenz and I sat down on the bench outside of Farley because we had survived and we were talking about how wonderful the year was going to be. And then she said, "I have a confession to make." I said, "What's that?" She said, "I've got to tell you that when they said I was going to be paired up with this gung-ho black woman law student, I was pretty nervous."

And I said, "When they told me I was going to be paired up with some *nun,*

Opposite: Ann Claire Williams (third from left) with other law school students, 1974.

"The first time I was at a football game and I heard the fight song and I heard the women singing, 'While her loyal sons *and daughters* are marching to victory,' to me that was also a moment because Notre Dame *does* have loyal sons and daughters."

so was I!" That began a lifelong friendship and a great interaction and perspective that I always remember about Notre Dame. It broadened me. It exposed me to so many different kinds of people, particularly working in an undergraduate hall. I felt like I was a part of that spirit and participated in groundbreaking history for women. I often think about that conversation that we had, how Notre Dame is a place where those kinds of relationships could blossom.

I come back to the university on a regular basis because I'm the secretary on the board of trustees. The first time I was at a football game and I heard the fight song and I heard the women singing, "While her loyal sons *and daughters* are marching to victory," to me that was also a moment because Notre Dame *does* have loyal sons and daughters. So it also struck me that women felt that they were part of the loyal sons and daughters. The fight song hasn't changed yet; officially it's still just "loyal sons," but I'm not giving up on that.

To incoming freshmen, I would say: Be open to meeting new and different people, open to diversity. Do not cling to all the values and people that you have just spent your whole life with. This is an opportunity to reach out to others who come from different backgrounds. We're all richer for knowing different kinds of people, of different races, of different religions. College is the time to form those friendships, because they will be lifelong friendships.

Honorable Ann Claire Williams was the first African American to be appointed to the United States Court of Appeals for the Seventh Circuit. "Notre Dame instills in you that obligation that you owe something back," she says. "The whole 'Do unto others as you would have done unto you.' That part of the law school philosophy was part and parcel of your degree, that you had to go out into the world and try to do some good."

"Always be grateful for the opportunity to serve."

Reverend John I. Jenkins, C.S.C.

Class of 1976

Notre Dame taught me that the Catholic faith is a set of beliefs—plus a whole lot more. It's a lens through which you look at life, a language you speak, a set of appreciations, and the way you appreciate them. Even though I didn't have a spiritual awakening per se, because I was blessed by a family already energized by faith, the masses and all the beautiful signs and symbols of Catholic spiritual life at Notre Dame helped to keep me awake, even restless, you might say. As a philosophy major, I probed deeply into belief and unbelief, and occasionally I questioned my own faith, but the campus had—and still has—all the resources and traditions, all the people, places, and activities that help a person stay anchored and hopeful. Once you're on steady ground like that, and you're in a position to listen with gratitude and humility, God's going to keep

waking you up to new possibilities and next steps you can take. For me, those wake-up calls led me to the Holy Cross priesthood and the embrace of philosophical ideas that can make our faith still more alive.

I was blessed with many good friends, with whom I had scores of great conversations, during my years as part of the class of '76. Not surprisingly, I've continued to benefit greatly from the influence of many fellow Domers, but I feel compelled right now to mention someone whose message, if you will, has stuck in my mind even though he graduated ahead of me. I did not know him personally, and we only exchanged a few words over the years. Al Sondej was a witness to me and my classmates about the poor, about the

Sermon on the Mount. He worked in the dining hall, making his own meal from the leftovers. Every day, he stood outside the dining hall at mealtime, collecting change from students to help feed the world's hungry. He never took on a judgmental air or an air of moral superiority. He was always smiling and thankful for our quarters. Seeing him every day taught me what it means to have a vocation and to offer witness simply and quietly.

For words of wisdom, I pass along the words that my father relayed to me, quoting his own father: Always be grateful for the opportunity to serve. This advice might not have originated

Opposite: Father Jenkins celebrating with students at the student ball, the evening of his inauguration, 2005.

"God's going to keep waking you up to new possibilities
and next steps you can take."

from the lips of a Domer, but I certainly have seen people all over campus demonstrating it and teaching it by example throughout the years. This was true of my student days and equally true when I joined the Holy Cross community. Father Ted Hesburgh, Father Edmund "Ned" Joyce, Father Charlie Sheedy, and many others helped me aspire to be a priest dedicated to service. Now, with the opportunities for services that come with the presidency of this great university, and with the opportunity that this university has to serve the nation and the world, I want to recall—and pass along—my father's advice more than ever.

Opposite: Father Jenkins at his inauguration as the seventeenth president of the University of Notre Dame, 2005.

Reverend John I. Jenkins, C.S.C., became the University of Notre Dame's seventeenth president on July 1, 2005. A professor of philosophy at the University, Father Jenkins was religious superior of the Holy Cross priests and brothers at Notre Dame from 1997 to 2000. A member of the Notre Dame faculty since 1990 and the recipient of a Lilly Teaching Fellowship in 1991–92, Father Jenkins teaches in the areas of ancient philosophy, medieval philosophy, and the philosophy of religion. He is the author of Knowledge and Faith in Thomas Aquinas, *published by Cambridge University Press in 1997. Prior to joining the Congregation of Holy Cross, he earned bachelor's and master's degrees in philosophy from Notre Dame in 1976 and '78, respectively. Father Jenkins was ordained a priest in the Basilica of the Sacred Heart on campus in 1983.*

"Life isn't fair, so get used to it."

Daniel "Rudy" Ruettiger

Class of 1976

When I grew up as a little boy, Notre Dame meant a lot to my family. It meant a lot to the blue-collar ethnic group where we grew up. We were as conservative Catholic as you could get. Basically Notre Dame meant, to me, school spirit. And when I first stepped on campus, that's what I felt. The confusion of my past went away. It made me focus on what I needed to do to get me to Notre Dame and make me stay there. Because it was such a strong feeling of "I belong here as well as anyone else."

I think that's what takes everybody to the next level: a sense of confidence. You can't look in the mirror and say, "Well, I'm not sure if I can make it." When you have confidence, there's a different look in that mirror. And that

Opposite: Daniel "Rudy" Ruettiger was the inspiration behind the TriStar movie *Rudy*.

comes from proving to yourself, through preparation, and seeing yourself where you have to be. And you have to keep reality in mind. As in: Life isn't fair. So get used to it. And I got used to that.

One of the things in a Catholic education—I grew up with a Catholic education—we had great teachers, great nuns. It's very strict and they don't take any nonsense, but unfortunately they don't understand learning disorders. I had been diagnosed with dyslexia, but back then, I was "uncoachable" and "untrainable." And I wasn't slow. I was ahead of the game. But I just couldn't sit there and pay attention in class. And the instructor would say that I wasn't paying attention. But the thing was, I didn't want to listen to the teachers that were making me feel bad.

But no matter what they said to me and what they said I could never be, I just found out a way to get there. It was great preparation for me because Notre

Daniel "Rudy" Ruettiger, wearing number 45, being carried off the field after playing against Georgia Tech, and winning 24–3, in the only game he ever played, on November 8, 1975.

Dame was tough on me. The tougher Notre Dame was on me as a student, the better I became as a person and a student. I came to practice every day like I was supposed to play. That's that preparation that I was talking about. See, I expected to play.

The greatest speech I was ever given, you see a little of it in the movie. Sean Astin is standing in the tunnel looking out in the field, and he says, "I quit," and the janitor says to him, "What do you mean, you quit? Shouldn't you be out at practice?" And he says, "No, I quit. They lied to me. They told me they were going to suit me and they didn't suit me. It's not worth it. All the hard work I put in, everything I did, wasn't worth it." And that's when the reality check came in: It *is* worth it. Because you're not dressing doesn't mean you didn't win. Because you're not going to walk through the tunnel doesn't mean you didn't win. That's life, dude, you know? You do not get what you want. You gotta move forward. But look at all of what you have done. You got to go to a university that everyone said you would never be at, and you're going to graduate from Notre Dame. You have a degree from Notre Dame.

And then the moment I got in the game, I expected it. That was no big deal. Here's the key to all dreams: When you have a dream that you end up with, they go real quick and they don't last. When it happened, it was more of a "Thank God I never quit. I almost quit."

So you have to wake up every morning and know that things are not going to go the way you want them to go. Life isn't fair, so get used to it. You better get used to that, but you better adjust to it through a positive attitude. How do you get a positive attitude? Well, my answer to that is that you have to be connected

Daniel "Rudy" Ruettiger, 1976, *Dome Yearbook*.

"There's only one Joe Montana. But there's millions of Rudys."

and have that purpose in anything you do. If you're not passionate or excited about what you're doing, it's easy to quit. It's easy to give up. It's better to say, "Hey, this is what I want. This is what's going to happen." A do-or-die type of attitude.

People see me today and say, "Oh, you're lucky. You've got a good life." And they ask me to tell them something about football. And I say that I really can't, because I only played for twenty-seven seconds. It was more about the journey.

I get e-mails from India and Australia saying how the movie's inspired them to be better people. So you know they're not looking at it as a football movie, whereas some people were looking at it as "Well, Rudy didn't do anything. He

only made one tackle. He's not a Joe Montana." I always say to people that there's only one Joe Montana. But there's millions of Rudys. There's millions of Rudys—so get used to that.

Daniel "Rudy" Ruettiger was the inspiration for the TriStar movie Rudy. *Ruettiger is a motivational speaker and founder of Rudy International. He has co-authored several books and has produced a motivational tape series called* Dream Power. *In 1997, he established the Rudy Foundation, whose mission is to help children of all ages around the world reach their full potential. He was, at the time, the only football player in Notre Dame's history to be carried off the field on his teammates' shoulders.*

> ## "Faith and family are more important than your job."
>
> **Charlie Weis**
> Class of 1978

Growing up Catholic in New Jersey, Notre Dame was a very popular school. They used to have those Notre Dame highlights with Lindsey Nelson. Really, you used to schedule what time you'd go to church around Notre Dame highlights. I didn't know where South Bend, Indiana, was. When I was a junior in high school, I was paging through a college directory, and it was the first school that had all the things I was looking for.

I used to love going to Breen-Phillips for eleven o'clock mass on Sunday night. It was one of my favorite things in the entire week to do. You're always studying. Sunday night you're always struggling to get caught up academically, and you leave the library at about quarter to eleven and walk over to mass. The place would be standing room only because it would be the last

Charlie Weis, 1978, *Dome Yearbook.*

mass on campus—you know, everyone having slept in on Sunday. I used to really enjoy that. It was always a fun mass. The priest always used to make fun of taking collections because nobody ever had any money. It was really a feel-good time and it would always lead to some deep philosophical discussions on Sunday night after we'd go back to the dorm, whether they were on the homily or something political that was related to something at mass. It was one of my favorite times of the week.

You always have to keep a perspective that faith and family are more important than your job. I think that very few people live by that rule. If I had something that I had to do for my family which meant quitting here today, I would quit here today without blinking an eye. And most people can't do that. Most people put the job in the pecking order as more important than their family and faith. And you can't live that way. You watched it when you were growing up, with your own parents, the sacrifices they made as you were growing up. Once you have kids, you realize

> "Once you can suppress your ego and put it on the back burner, I think you have a much better chance of being more fulfilled in life."

that you really don't matter anymore. Really, it's how you can take care of your wife and your kids that is more important than your own ego. Once you can suppress your ego and put it on the back burner, I think you have a much better chance of being more fulfilled in life. I'm the big man on campus here, but when I go home, I'm the low man in the pecking order.

Charlie Weis is the head football coach at Notre Dame. He owns four Super Bowl rings. During his Notre Dame years, he never played football.

Charlie Weis on Notre Dame campus, 2005.

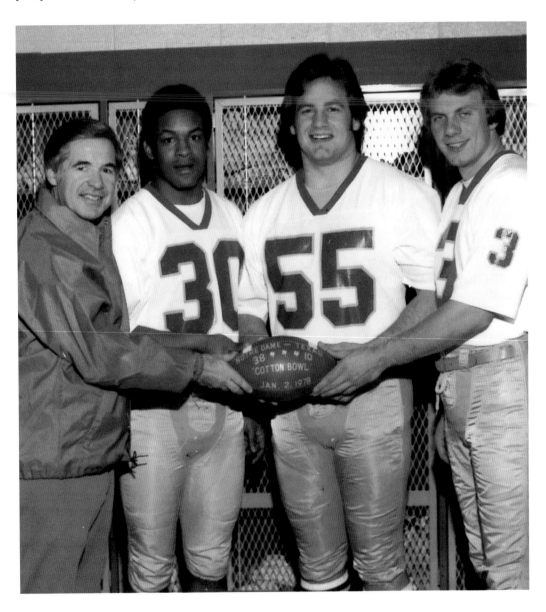

house and call your house and disrupt things. What do you think I should do?" She said, "I'll be honest with you. I think you should go to Notre Dame." To this day, that was the best advice anyone ever gave me. I tip my hat to her.

When I eventually left St. Louis I said, "Look, Mom, I'm moving to big-time Chicago. I'm going to take my trophies and my plaques and my diploma." She said, "I'll tell you what, you can have all your personal belongings, but the trophies and diploma stay here." So my diploma is still at my mother's house in St. Louis!

You know, the first time I carried a ball at Notre Dame, I fumbled! At Boston College. Then I looked up almost four years later, and I broke George Gipp's career rushing record. People probably remember me on the football field, but my biggest thing is I loved all sports. I remember days after practice, I would go into the basketball gym and just sit there on the team bench and

Opposite: Coach Devine with captains Heavens, Golic, and Montana, 1978.

"That's the greatest thing for me to say right now, that I am a graduate of Notre Dame."

say, "Hey, Digger Phelps, give me a chance!" It was just an opportunity to be around great athletes, playing with some of the greatest ballplayers in the world.

That's the greatest thing for me to say right now, that I am a graduate of Notre Dame. I kind of walk around with my chest out, but I'm not thin like I used to be. But I make it a point to get back and let those guys know that I am still a part of them in a sense. I just bleed Notre Dame every day.

Jerome Heavens, who was tri-captain, broke The Gipper's Notre Dame rushing record in 1978. Heavens's freshman rushing record of 756 yards was only recently surpassed by Darius Walker.

"Don't ever admit someone's better than you."

Joe Montana

Class of 1979

I hate to lose more than I like to win. I think it was avoiding that feeling of losing that really drove me more than anything. When you win, it's okay. That's what I was supposed to do. When you win, you take a breath and go on to next week, whereas losing is that feeling like when your adrenaline just goes away. That feeling, I hate. The games I remember more are the ones we lost. The last USC game really kills me. Paul McDonald ducked to avoid the pass rush and he dropped the ball and they called it an incomplete pass. The next play they throw a 25–30 yard pass down the middle, time out, and they kicked a field goal with two or three seconds left, and we lost, 27–25. I was driven by the hate of failure.

At the 1979 Cotton Bowl, we came back to win, but there were so many things that happened in that game. I

watched the end of it with my boys recently on ESPN Classics. They said, "Daddy, is this the game you came back to win?" I said, "Yeah, but watch. I try to give it away two or three times before the game is over."

That's why I tell my boys that you can never give up. If you go look in history, especially with me, if I thought about the play that just happened, it would have been impossible for me to win. The play before the big catch at the Cotton Bowl, I misread Kris Haines by three feet. He was standing there—he would have walked into the end zone. I know I fumbled twice at least. There were sixty-nine points scored, and only fourteen were scored against the wind. And one was a blocked punt returned for a touchdown.

But I have the strange ability to not think about the play prior to the one I'm in. Some guys can remember games from twenty or thirty years ago—the whole game. I can't even remember the

Opposite: Joe Montana during a game against Missouri, 1978.

"No matter how much it takes, you always have to prepare yourself as if you're the starter."

Joe Montana in a Notre Dame game, late 1970s.

score, let alone the plays. I was always able to put things behind me quickly.

Another important thing to think about is preparation. That's probably one of the best pieces of advice I can give someone. No matter how much it takes, you always have to prepare yourself as if you're the starter. I think that's the biggest key. Guys who don't succeed really aren't ready when it's their chance. You just never know when your chance is going to come. So whether you're first team or third team, it doesn't really matter. You still have to be as prepared as the guy who's playing.

And there's something I said recently to one of my boys: "Look, I don't care if you think some other kid is better than you. I don't care if you think his arm is better than your arm. Don't ever admit it. And if he beats you five times in a row, challenge him to a sixth time." Don't ever admit someone's better than you. You put yourself in a defeated position before you even get an opportunity to show what you can do. I always said, "You may beat me down, but I'm still going to come back. I'm going to beat you this time and the next time until you begin to believe that I'll beat you, and the people around you believe it, too."

Joe Montana is a former quarterback for the San Francisco 49ers and has won four Super Bowl championships. In the 1979 Cotton Bowl game, Joe was suffering from hypothermia and drinking chicken broth in the second half, right before he threw the famous pass to Kris Haines. Notre Dame won the game, 35–34. He is also the author of the motivational book The Winning Spirit: 16 Timeless Principles That Drive Performance Excellence *(Random House, 2005).*

"Being able to reach your goals at such a prestigious university—that really makes you believe in yourself."

Dr. Carol Lally Shields

Class of 1979

Professor Emil T. Hoffman would give these Friday quizzes, but he would never give a quiz without having someone proofread it, because he made a lot of little errors. He was kind of like an absentminded professor. So he wanted to ask my roommate Liz Berry to proofread his quizzes the day before ... but Emil was smart. He knew he couldn't just have Liz do it, because she had two roommates who would find out about it—so he asked *all three* of us to be his proofreaders. My whole freshman year, I knew every question on the test the day before the test, every week. I could have probably made a million dollars selling those questions to the freshmen if they wanted to know the test ahead of time! But we kept our

Opposite: Dr. Lally Shields examining a sedated baby with eye cancer at Wills Eye Hospital.

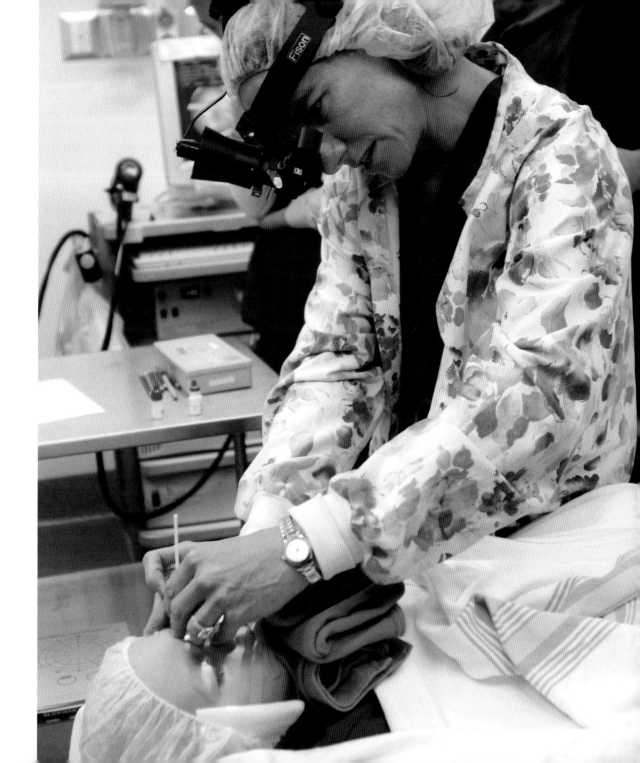

"Everybody was always amazed that we
were so easygoing about Emil's tests. Little
did they know we already took it!"

Carol Lally, 1978.

mouths shut and would pretend like we were studying chemistry every Thursday night.

Everybody was always amazed that we were so easygoing about Emil's tests. Little did they know we already took it! On Fridays, we had to go in and pretend like we were using our slide rules to calculate the answers. That had an enormous impact on me. It was like, "Emil T. thinks I'm kind of special, so I'm okay. I can keep up."

The kind of work I do now is very precise and we handle potentially fatal cancers that can occur on or in the eye. Many of them occur in kids' eyes. As I'm operating in kids' eyes, and using little lasers that are only like three or four millimeters from their central vision,

Carol Lally with mother and father, Dr. and Mrs. Francis Lally, on Graduation Day, 1979.

"You have to be really focused, and you have to be confident in yourself to do this kind of work."

I'm thinking, "If someone bumps me at this point, this kid's central vision is knocked out for good." You have to be really focused, and you have to be confident in yourself to do this kind of work. I was able to reach my goals at such a prestigious university—that really makes you believe in yourself. We see a lot of patients, and they come in from long distances to see a specialist who can help them with the most important problem in their life, this cancer that could kill their child or could blind them. I've got incredible endurance to do this kind of work, and I get incredible satisfaction at work. Every day, we save two or three more lives. What more can you ask for?

Carol Lally Shields, M.D., is co-director of the ocular oncology service at Wills Eye Hospital in Philadelphia. She lives in a Philadelphia suburb with her husband and their seven children. At Notre Dame she played basketball and was the first female student-athlete to receive the Byron Kanaley Award for excellence in academics and leadership, the highest honor given to Notre Dame student-athletes.

Students on campus, circa 1960s.

"Come, Holy Spirit."

Reverend Ted Hesburgh, C.S.C.

Honorary L.L.D., 1984

On August 13, 1935, I got the habit and twelve months later and a day, on the sixteenth of August in 1936, I took vows of poverty, chastity, and obedience for three years. And then I came back to Notre Dame and started a new semester in September, my second year. That year I lived at Moreau Seminary on the other lake. That was a busy year, a lot going on. I did fairly well there.

When I was a kid, I was interested in words—big words. I remember when I saw a word that I didn't understand, I looked it up, studied it, wrote it down, and then I tried to use it two or three times the next week.

Opposite: Father Hesburgh in September 2005, at the inauguration of Rev. John I. Jenkins, C.S.C, the seventeenth president of the University of Notre Dame.

So my writing was fairly good except that my vocabulary was a little too lengthy in words. I'll never forget, we had a class in the history of English literature. It was a wonderful, wonderful class taught by a priest in our community. I always loved English and I loved writing. We had a final paper, and the mark you got on your final paper was the mark that you got for the course. I went up with great anticipation to get this paper and I glanced down. In big red numbers, there was a 96, which was pretty good in those days.

Then I noticed some handwriting across the top of the paper. He said, "If you don't learn to use monosyllabic words, you're going to wind up being a monumental bore." I thought that was pretty good advice. And that was the end of the big words! I remembered glorying in the fact that one of my favorite poems only had two polysyllabic words. The rest were all monosyllables. "The woods are lovely, dark and deep / But I have promises to keep / And miles to go before I sleep." That's Robert Frost.

One of the best things I did at Notre

"She happens also to be the Mother of God, so I find it a bit inconceivable that in Her university She looks down and all She sees is men."

Dame, and this was startling around here given our long history and our male tradition, was saying, "It's rather inconceivable to have a great university named after the Mother of God who happens to be a woman and to have all men students. It's masculine. It's like a gym. I said, "It's high time we admitted women as students, professors, administrators, everything." Of course, that came as a bit of a shock to the old boys. But we had a meeting for a whole week and the old boys had a chance to argue. I just sat there and let them talk.

At the end, I just said, "Look, we got a university named after a woman who happens to be the greatest human person that ever lived. Jesus was not a human first. He was a divine person with a human nature. She happens to be the greatest human person that ever lived and she happens to be a woman, and this school happens to be named after her. She happens also to be the Mother of God, so I find it a bit inconceivable that in Her university She looks down and all She sees is men. I suspect she's interested in women getting this kind of education." I won. The vote on that was, I remember, thirty-nine to six. So I think that was pretty good support. It made a lot of sense. I can tell you that it's a much better place today because half of the people here are women. If you have all men in the place, it gets to be either like a zoo or a gym, and both are not very civilized. I think that women have added a great dimension here.

My advice is that life is full of problems and you need help. The greatest help you can get is to go back to the gospel, when the Lord was leaving the apostles and He said, "I'm not going to leave you men orphans. I'm going to send you the Holy Spirit and He'll inspire you on what to say, what to do, and how to do it." I say get in the habit of the shortest prayer I know, which is the best, and that's "Come, Holy Spirit." I do it in Latin, "Veni, Sancti Spiritus," because it's a throwback to my studying days.

Father Ted Hesburgh, circa 1940.

"My advice is that life is full of problems, and you need help."

And that's not just for classes, not just for your personal life, but that's for everything in life. I say it the first thing in the morning and many times during the day, because you're constantly running into situations where you don't know the answer or you're trying to write something and you can't get through a block there. I say it and it never fails: I've got the greatest intelligence in the universe. The Lord says, "I'm giving this to you. I'm not going to leave you orphans." Just call on this wisdom, and you've got all the help you need. You not only get intelligence, but you get the strength to do it.

Opposite: Father Hesburgh (back row) with family at Lake Ontario, 1943.

Intelligence is great. I know a lot of things I *should* do, but I don't necessarily *do* them. I also need the grace to act on what I know. Life and strength, that's what I tell these students. They come back later and say they're still saying "Come, Holy Spirit" ten times a day and it still helps them out. It's a simple bit of advice, but it's very good advice.

The desk where I work is next to a window. I just have to turn and look out the window, and what's out there is Our Lady on the Dome. I can almost reach out and touch Her, but She's a quarter of a mile away maybe. If I'm stuck with something, I say, "Lady, it's your place and we're in deep trouble and you've got to get us out of it." And She does. Those students are not praying at the Grotto simply because it's an

attractive place. It's a place where you can pray and it's a place where you look up and remind yourself that Mary came down there to talk to those peasants and lords. If I'm writing something and I need a little breakthrough, I just look out and say, "I'm going to need some help on this one." It's a reminder that it's Her place and She's here. It's very palpable. She's always shining, and She's always there.

Reverend Theodore M. Hesburgh, C.S.C., is president emeritus of the University of Notre Dame, having led the university for thirty-five years. He is author of the national bestseller God, Country, Notre Dame *(also published by Doubleday). During his time as a student, Father Hesburgh practiced a year of silence in 1936, "from August to August." Twenty-nine candidates began that year with him and seven came out. "They don't have that kind of year anymore," says Father Hesburgh. "Guys probably wouldn't last."*

Father Hesburgh (middle row, second from right) at his ordination, 1943.

"There's nothing like an honest connection with nature."

Richard Webb McDaniel

Class of 1984

The first night game in Notre Dame history took place in 1982, against Michigan. It was my first year as a graduate student in fine arts. After a delicious Wolverine burger, I joined the enthusiastic crowd that accompanied the band across campus to the stadium. I entered the appropriate gate and filed in toward the stands, amazed at the electrifying brilliance of the illuminated field. Soon I realized there was something vastly different in the way Notre Dame students watched a football game in South Bend.

Instead of sitting down during the game and standing to stretch during halftime, the common practice was just the opposite. We stood up on top of the seats during the game, even jumping up and down with varying degrees of caution, and did not sit until halftime. This is just the way it was done at ND—rain or shine or snowstorm.

"I am still amazed how strong the pull of nature can be."

Richard Webb McDaniel, M.F.A., 1984.

A place that has special meaning for me personally, though, is St. Joseph's Lake. Sure, it's a great place for a romantic walk or for a healthy run, perhaps a figure eight around both lakes, St. Joseph's and St. Mary's. But my clearest memory of the lake was the day I decided to take my drawing class out to draw trees. I was a graduate assistant on scholarship and taught a class in basic drawing. The day was gorgeous and I invited the class out to the lake. You see, one of the challenges for beginners is to avoid being overwhelmed by all the detail in the landscape: too many leaves, too many twigs, too many branches. So I took the class to the lake and told them to draw any trees they wanted—on the other side of the lake. This is a time-tested technique for simplification through distance.

What made the day memorable was that I got into trouble (deservedly so) for taking the class out "on location" without filing a proper flight plan. It was an innocent mistake, and I understood my advisor's concern as he reprimanded me, suggesting that I always make a class report back to the classroom for roll call after such an excursion. Otherwise, he reasoned, they were free to run off once they were outside of my direct control. I tried to hide my internal smile, for the whole time I was being scolded I knew that not a single student had left the class early. They must have been suitably impressed with the beauty of the lake and the thrill of drawing or painting outdoors.

I have been painting *en plein air* ever since, even when direct landscape painting was unpopular with the critics, and I still am amazed how strong the pull of nature can be. In fact, my latest book, *On Location,* describes the very same impulses that first drew me to St. Joseph's Lake. There's nothing like an honest connection with nature.

Richard Webb McDaniel, M.F.A. 1984, was born in Berkeley, California. For nearly two decades, while living in the artistically rich Hudson River Valley, he painted and taught at the Woodstock School of Art. Now back in his home state, Richard paints, teaches national workshops, and recently completed his fifth book: On Location: Plein Air Painting in Pastel.

Saratoga : Spring, **1988; oil on canvas, 30" x 44".**

"If you're going to do something, be in it 100 percent."

Mike Golic

Class of 1985

My freshman year when we beat LSU in the opening game, we vaulted to number one in the country. I had visions of major bowl games and national championships dancing in my head. Then we go to the big house in Michigan and get *smoked*. You hear that line "Losing builds character"? Well, there's only so much character you want built. After a while, you're just putting too many bricks in the foundation! I probably am the cliché of "I'm still glad I went there for the experience because I love Notre Dame," but there's no way I'm going to sit there and say, "Well, the losing helped me build character." That's bull. I wanted to *win*. I'm sorry we didn't win.

My sophomore year, we went to Pittsburgh, and Pittsburgh was ranked number one in the country. That was Allen Pinkett's freshman year. It was when Dan Marino was there. They were

"You hear that line 'Losing builds character'?
Well, there's only so much character you want built."

7–0, and we went to Pittsburgh and we *smoked* them. I remembered when the buses brought us back to Notre Dame and we turned down Notre Dame Avenue. The streets were packed with students going nuts because we just knocked off the number-one team in the country. I thought to myself, "This is why I'm at Notre Dame." The students were jumping in the *windows* of the bus. It was the best single moment I had there. I'll never forget it. I thought that I'd have a lot of moments like that, but it turned out there'd only be one.

After playing nine years in the NFL, I can honestly say there was no feeling I had in the NFL that matched running out of the tunnel at Notre Dame. There's nothing that matched that chill that I got when I was standing in the tunnel getting ready to run out and all of a sudden the students started pouring on the field to make the human tunnel for you to run through. Before that, coming down the steps and touching the sign "Play Like a Champion Today," there was nothing like that. I didn't experience that in the NFL. If I had played in the Super Bowl, I may have, but I didn't. So football-wise, that was still the best feeling I had: standing in the tunnel at Notre Dame. Every single game—it was an unbelievable, electric feeling. If you're going to do something, be in it 100 percent.

Mike Golic is co-host of Mike & Mike in the Morning *on ESPN 103.3 FM, and is also an analyst for ESPN and ESPN2's NFL studio programming and college football game coverage. He met his future wife (who went to Saint Mary's College) on the first day of school at Notre Dame, while walking to a freshman orientation dance.*

Opposite: Mike Golic, early 1980s.

"Experiencing the death of a dream forces you to grow up."

Nicholas Sparks

Class of 1988

I went to Notre Dame on a track scholarship, and I got injured right off the bat, freshman year in the cross-country season—it was my Achilles, I had tendonitis. But I came back for the track season and I broke the school record. That was one of the great experiences of my life—and it's something that I still think back on today. We were at the Drake Relays. The team was very strong and I was the third leg. I got the baton in second place and finished in second place. I had no idea how fast I ran because everybody runs half a mile, so you don't know how fast you really run. We finished in third place. We were very happy. The coach was jumping up and down shouting out times. It wasn't until I came back that I saw the board and saw that we broke the school record.

The next year, when I was a sophomore, I injured my Achilles again. This

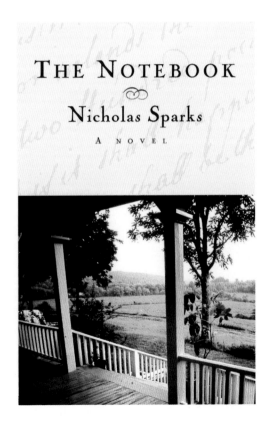

time it was much worse. I ended up having surgery on it in March. From August through March, I had struggled. I would run a little bit and the injury would come back. I would go to a race on crutches, then throw the crutches down and race and get on my crutches again. If I lifted my foot down and up you'd hear a squeak, like a loud door squeak. My Achilles was like a golf ball. The doctor had said, "You can't run for eight weeks. You just can*not* run." I think any success I had in writing came from what I learned in athletics. Writing is all about perseverance and discipline. If you have enough perseverance and discipline, you can do a little better than those with a lot of talent.

I've always been really driven. I was

"I think any success I had in writing came
from what I learned in athletics."

the valedictorian of my high school. I worked full time. I had a girlfriend . . . and I still got a full scholarship. I was driven ever since I was a little kid. Notre Dame was the first time I ever experienced failure. I remember when it finally came time to quit. I ended up having to get cortisone shots in the bottom of my foot to train. I was able to run for two months, but then the pain came back. I was down to getting a cortisone shot every ten days just so I could train. I remember walking out my senior year. I had my spikes on. I just stood there, looked at the track, and said, "I can't do this anymore." I've got to walk for the rest of my life. I talked to my coach and said, "Look, I'm physically unable. I'm injured."

That was the first time I'd ever failed. That was very hard. That was probably the biggest dream I've ever had in my life, much bigger than writing. It was the dream of going to the Olympics. You give that up, and it hurts. You feel your dream beginning to die. You lie there knowing that everyone else is out there training and you're falling behind every day that you miss. For me, it started my freshman year, when I got injured. So I'm moping. And my mom said, "Look, don't just pout. Do something." I said, "Like what?" She said, "I don't know. Write a book." Just like that. I had never considered it. So I said, "Okay." I had nothing else to do. I grabbed a Smith Corona typewriter and typed out a novel. It took about

Nicholas Sparks, 1984.
Opposite: Administration Building, 2000.

eight weeks. This wasn't *The Note-book*—*The Notebook* was my fourth attempt.

The death of a dream brings into question your own thoughts about reality, about what you can really do. And it's always not what you dreamed you could do. It's different. Experiencing the death of a dream forces you to grow up. I lived through the death of a dream. If that's the worst that could happen, that feeling, I'd lived through that already. After that, I really felt I could try anything.

Nicholas Sparks is the bestselling author of The Notebook, Message in a Bottle, *and* A Walk to Remember, *among others, and his newest book is* At First Sight. *Sparks lives in North Carolina with his wife and five children. He is a major contributor to the Creative Writing MFA program at Notre Dame—his contributions provide scholarships, internships, and a fellowship each year.*

"Recognize and embrace your talents, especially if they lie outside the typical idea of what will bring success."

Casey Dame

Class of 1992

I was originally a Biology major at Notre Dame, despite my innate artistic abilities. I succumbed to the popular notion that only scientists and engineers are "smart" and have prestigious careers. Luckily, I recognized in time that my passion had always been art, and I was denying the gift I'd been given by not committing to my talents. I switched majors and knew it was the right decision. Each instructor gave me insight and words of wisdom:

Professor Douglas Kinsey said good art is based on the artist's own personal experiences. As an artist, you have an obligation to learn constantly about every subject and every situation you encounter.

Professor Donald Vogl told me it takes twenty years to become just a "good" artist. Good advice for a young

Casey Dame, 1992, *Dome Yearbook*.

ambitious artist. Father Austin Collins was brutally honest when it came to critiques. He was never unnecessarily harsh, but he took very seriously the development of students' talents. This taught me how to make an honest assessment of my own work and how to improve it.

Being an Art major at a conservative university does have some slight drawbacks, though. I would get quizzical and somewhat disappointed reactions from people who asked my major. I think there is a general perception that being a Studio Arts major means something akin to making macaroni necklaces or

"As an artist, you have an obligation to
learn constantly about every subject and
every situation you encounter."

macramé potholders. Deciding to fol-
low my passion for art instead of taking
the road conventional wisdom advised
was the decision that set me up for
where I am today, and where I will be
tomorrow.

For incoming freshmen, I would
advise you to recognize and embrace
your talents, especially if they lie outside the typical idea of what will bring
success.

*Casey Dame is an animator and charac-
ter technical director for feature films,
including* The Chronicles of Narnia: The
Lion, the Witch, and the Wardrobe;
Charlie and the Chocolate Factory; *and*
The Lord of the Rings: The Return of the
King. *He met and married his wife while
at Notre Dame.*

"If you prepare yourself, you can do the best you can. The games you beat yourself up on are the games you don't feel like you were prepared for."

Ruth Riley

Class of 2001

Notre Dame was the only school that I visited. I was actually pretty shy in high school and I knew that I wanted to stay close to home—and my sister was there; she was a year ahead of me. I visited Notre Dame, and once I stepped on campus I knew that was where I wanted to go. I just felt like I could be at home there. Especially with the basketball staff, because that was who I was going to spend a lot of time with. I waited a while to tell Coach. She probably wished I could have told her sooner that I was coming!

Confidence is probably the biggest thing that I gained in college. I was pretty soft-spoken and quiet going in, and with basketball I was thrown into the spotlight, you could say. I was being interviewed for the first time. It was kind of an eye-opening experience after my freshman year. At the end of the

"I started gaining confidence, not only in my basketball ability but in who I could become."

freshman year, we had gone through the tournament and probably made it further than most people expected and had played better than most people probably expected. At that point I realized that something special could happen in the future. I started gaining confidence, not only in my basketball ability but in who I could become.

But that first interview, it was horrible. It was like one-word answers. I was an interviewer's nightmare. My teammates still give me a hard time about it!

Obviously the end of that one game [in 2001] was probably the biggest turning point for me. Getting fouled

Opposite: Ruth Riley (center), circa 2000.

and then going to the free-throw line and having to make those two free throws … It was a tie game and we had the ball, so Coach draws a little play for me. Our floor was supposed to get me the ball any way she could, so she just draws it up there and says, "Go get it and get fouled." It's funny because at 66–66, it's a tie game and people are all like, "Are you nervous?" and I'm like, "Not really." I mean, how many free throws have I shot in my life? It's not like I wasn't prepared for it. It's not like a shot I've never taken before. I'm like the kind of player who's going to prepare myself as best I can for every situation and I felt like I had done enough to prepare myself for that. I know in some ways I'm not going to be the most tal-

"I mean, how many free throws have I shot in my life?
It's not like I wasn't prepared for it."

ented, the most gifted. I feel like if you prepare yourself, you can do the best you can. The games you beat yourself up on are the games you don't feel like you were prepared for. Those are the games that stick in your mind, where you know you could have done more.

Ruth Riley is the center for the WNBA's Detroit Shock. She was on the 2004 U.S. women's Olympic basketball team, which won the gold medal in Athens. She holds Notre Dame's all-time blocked shot record with 370 and is the only Notre Dame player to have reached 2,000 points and 1,000 rebounds.

Ruth Riley, 2001, *Dome Yearbook.*
Opposite: Students on campus, 1970s.

STORIN

50. Courtesy of Matthew V. Storin
52. Courtesy of University of Notre Dame Archives

DWYRE

55. Courtesy of *Los Angeles Times*
56. Courtesy of University of Notre Dame Archives

KERNAN

59. Courtesy of University of Notre Dame
60. Courtesy of University of Notre Dame Archives

HANRATTY

62. Courtesy of Alex von Kleydorff
64–65. Courtesy of University of Notre Dame Archives

SCENIC

67. Stadium. Courtesy of University of Notre Dame Archives

NIGRO

68. Courtesy of Dr. Dennis M. Nigro
71. Courtesy of University of Notre Dame Archives

BROGAN

72. Courtesy of Michael Schwartz; www.mphotoart.com
74. Courtesy of University of Notre Dame Archives
77. Courtesy of University of Notre Dame Archives

JENKY

78. Courtesy of Bishop Daniel R. Jenky
81. Courtesy of Bishop Daniel R. Jenky
82. Courtesy of University of Notre Dame Archives

LIBOWITZ

84. Courtesy of Richard Libowitz
87. Courtesy of Richard Libowitz

SCENIC

88. Students on steps. Courtesy of University of Notre Dame Archives
89. Back of boys walking. Courtesy of University of Notre Dame Archives

THEISMANN

91. Courtesy of Michael and Susan Bennett, Lighthouse Imaging
93. Courtesy of University of Notre Dame Archives
94. Courtesy of University of Notre Dame Archives

MAURER

97. Courtesy of National Federation of the Blind
98. Courtesy of University of Notre Dame Archives

WILLIAMS

100. Courtesy of Honorable Ann Claire Williams
103. Courtesy of University of Notre Dame Archives

JENKINS

107. Courtesy of University of Notre Dame; Photographer: Matt Cashore
109. Courtesy of University of Notre Dame; Photographer: Matt Cashore
110. Courtesy of University of Notre Dame; Photographer: Matt Cashore

RUETTIGER

113. Courtesy of Daniel "Rudy" Ruettiger
114. Courtesy of University of Notre Dame Archives
116. Courtesy of University of Notre Dame Archives

SCENIC

118–119. Stadium. Matt Cashore

WEIS

121. Courtesy of Michael and Susan Bennett, Lighthouse Imaging
122. Courtesy of University of Notre Dame Archives
123. Courtesy of Michael and Susan Bennett, Lighthouse Imaging

HEAVENS

125. Courtesy of Jerome Heavens
126. Courtesy of University of Notre Dame Archives